# DOODLING FOR
# BOOKWORMS

## by Gemma Correll

This Library edition published in 2016 by Walter Foster Jr.,
an imprint of Quarto Publishing Group USA Inc.
6 Orchard Road, Suite 100
Lake Forest, CA 92630

Illustrated and written by Gemma Correll
Select text by Stephanie Carbajal

Distributed in the United States and Canada by
Lerner Publisher Services
241 First Avenue North
Minneapolis, MN 55401 U.S.A.
www.lernerbooks.com

First Library Edition

Library of Congress Cataloging-in-Publication Data

Names: Correll, Gemma, author, illustrator.
Title: Doodling for bookworms : inspiring doodle prompts and creative
   exercises for literature buffs / by Gemma Correll.
Description: Library [edition]. | Lake Forest : Walter Foster Publishing,
   2016.
Identifiers: LCCN 2015051212 | ISBN 9781942875086 (hardcover)
Subjects: LCSH: Books and reading in art. | Literature in art. |
   Drawing--Technique. | Doodles.
Classification: LCC NC915.D6 C677 2016 | DDC 745.8/39--dc23
LC record available at http://lccn.loc.gov/2015051212

Printed in USA
9 8 7 6 5 4 3 2 1

# TABLE OF CONTENTS

# HOW TO USE THIS BOOK

This book is just a guide. Each artist
has his or her own style. Using your imagination
will make the drawings more unique and special!
The fun of doodling comes from not trying too hard.
So don't worry about making mistakes or trying
to achieve perfection.

Here are some tips to help you get the
most of this book.

## DOODLE PROMPTS

The prompts in this book are designed to get your creative juices
flowing—and your pen and pencil moving! Don't think too much about
the prompts; just start drawing and see where your imagination takes
you. There's no such thing as a mistake in doodling!

## STEP-BY-STEP EXERCISES

Following the step-by-step exercises is fun and easy! The red lines
show you the next step. The black lines are the steps you've already
completed.

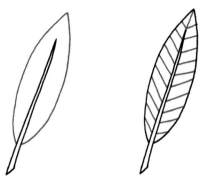

A. *Brideshead Revisited,* by Evelyn Waugh

B. *American Psycho,* by Bret Easton Ellis

C. *Great Expectations,* by Charles Dickens

D. *Catch-22,* by Joseph Heller

E. *Sense and Sensibility,* by Jane Austen

F. *Ulysses,* by James Joyce

G. *One Flew Over the Cuckoo's Nest,*
   by Ken Kesey

H. *The Catcher in the Rye,* by J.D. Salinger

I. *Crime and Punishment,* by Fyodor
   Dostoevsky

J. *A Wrinkle in Time,* by Madeleine L'Engle

1: F  2: C  3: H  4: A  5: I  6: B  7: D  8: E  9: G  10: J

# LITERARY HEROES & HEROINES

Some authors write very descriptively about the physical appearance of their characters. Others are more vague, leaving it up to the reader to imagine how a character might look.

Read the descriptions of characters from your favorite books and doodle them—where no description can be found, use your imagination!

Here are a few of my own doodles of famous heroes and heroines from literature to get you started.

ATTICUS FINCH
*To Kill a Mockingbird*
by Harper Lee

ELIZABETH BENNET
*Pride and Prejudice*
by Jane Austen

JO MARCH
*Little Women*
by Louisa May Alcott

**HESTER PRYNNE**
*The Scarlet Letter*
by Nathaniel Hawthorne

**OTHELLO**
*Othello*
by William Shakespeare

**HUCKLEBERRY FINN**
*The Adventures of Huckleberry Finn*
by Mark Twain

SAMUEL PICKWICK
*The Pickwick Papers*
by Charles Dickens

Try doodling some of your favorite heroes
and heroines.

# LITERARY VILLAINS & ANTI-HEROES

Of course some of the best characters in literature are not heroes at all, but anti-heroes or nasty villains!

Here are a few doodles of some of the greatest literary scoundrels and creeps.

**BILL SIKES**
*Oliver Twist*
by Charles Dickens

CRUELLA DE VIL
*101 Dalmatians*
by Dodie Smith

PINKIE BROWN
*Brighton Rock*
by Graham Greene

MRS. DANVERS
*Rebecca*
by Daphne duMaurier

THE THÉNARDIERS
*Les Misérables*
by Victor Hugo

PROFESSOR JAMES MORIARTY
*The Memoirs of Sherlock Holmes, "The Final Problem"*
by Sir Arthur Conan Doyle

Try doodling some of your favorite
literary villains.

# DRAW A BRILLIANT, BASIC BOOK

1. Draw two parallel lines, like this. The farther apart you draw them, the thicker your book will be.

This will be the spine of your book.

2. Join the lines at the top and bottom with slightly curved lines, like these.

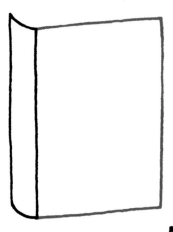

3. Draw three straight lines to form the cover of your book.

4. Then add another line at the top, like this.

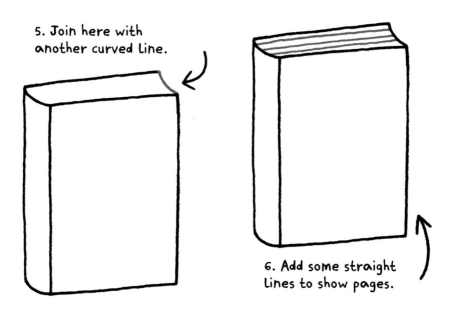

5. Join here with another curved line.

6. Add some straight lines to show pages.

THE CAT'S WHISKERS

7. Finally, decorate the cover of your book and add a title. Voilà!

# QUALITY QUOTES

A few of the cleverest, wittiest, and just all-around
wonderful quotes in literature...

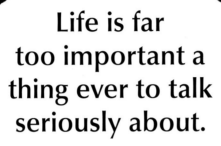

Life is far
too important a
thing ever to talk
seriously about.

Oscar Wilde
*Lady Windermere's Fan*

There is nothing I would
not do for those who are really
my friends. I have no notion of
loving people by halves; it is
not my nature.

Jane Austen
*Northanger Abbey*

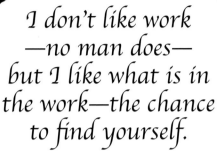

*I don't like work
—no man does—
but I like what is in
the work—the chance
to find yourself.*

Joseph Conrad
*Heart of Darkness*

Whenever you feel like
criticizing anyone...just
remember that all the people
in the world haven't had the
advantages that you've had.

F. Scott Fitzgerald
*The Great Gatsby*

Look at everything
always as though you
were seeing it either for the
first or last time:
Thus is your time on earth
filled with glory.

Betty Smith
*A Tree Grows in Brooklyn*

*Heaven knows we
need never be ashamed
of our tears, for they
are rain upon the blinding
dust of earth, overlying our
hard hearts.*

Charles Dickens
*Great Expectations*

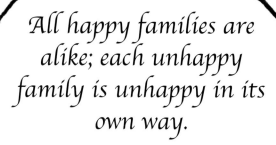

> *All happy families are alike; each unhappy family is unhappy in its own way.*
>
> Leo Tolstoy
> *Anna Karenina*

> **Definitions belong to the definers, not the defined.**
>
> Toni Morrison
> *Beloved*

# LITERARY CREATURES
## CATS

THE CHESHIRE CAT
*Alice's Adventures in Wonderland*
by Louis Carroll

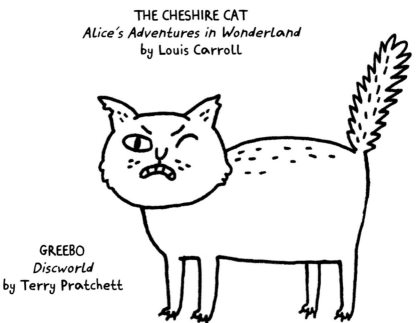

GREEBO
*Discworld*
by Terry Pratchett

# DOGS

MONTMORENCY — FOX TERRIER
*Three Men in a Boat*
by Jerome K. Jerome

WHITE FANG — 3/4 WOLF, 1/4 HUSKY
*White Fang*
by Jack London

# OTHER ANIMALS

WILBUR – PIG
CHARLOTTE – SPIDER
*Charlotte's Web*
by E.B. White

RATTY

TOAD

*The Wind in the Willows*
by Kenneth Grahame

# BIRDS

JONATHAN
LIVINGSTON SEAGULL
*Jonathan
Livingston Seagull*
by Richard Bach

THE LARK (that Juliet
insists is a Nightingale)
*Romeo and Juliet*
by William Shakespeare

Nevermore

THE RAVEN
"The Raven"
by Edgar Allan Poe

# DRAW A BASHFUL BOOKWORM

1. Draw a pair of glasses—two circles connected by a straight line.

2. Add eyes and a happy little mouth.

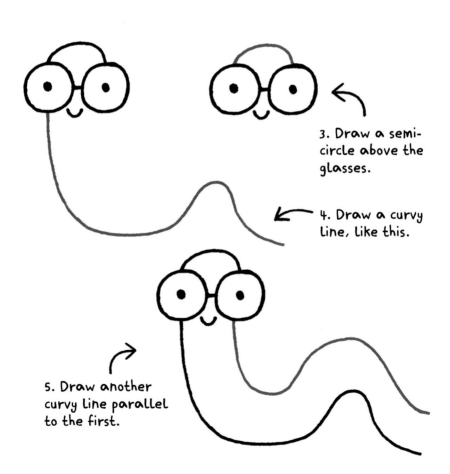

3. Draw a semi-circle above the glasses.

4. Draw a curvy line, like this.

5. Draw another curvy line parallel to the first.

6. Finish the bookworm's body with a curved shape.

7. Add color...what a beautiful bookworm!

Be sure to draw your bookworm something to read too.

# DRAW A TERRIFIC TYPEWRITER

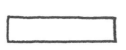

1. Start by drawing a rectangle.

2. Then add parallel curved lines at the top corners.

3. Add another rectangle at the top.

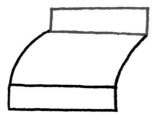

4. Draw three straight lines, like this, to make your typewriter look 3-D.

5. Draw a small rectangle for the space bar.

6. Draw little circles for the keys.*

*A standard typewriter has 46 keys (47 if you include the space bar), but just draw as many as you can fit—this is about fun, not accuracy!

7. Draw a semicircle, like this, for the typebars.

8. Then add a circle shape on the side. This bit is called the "platen knob."

9. Draw a piece of paper too, if you like.

Well done! What a terrific typewriter.

# BOOKMARKS

Just about anything can be a bookmark, especially at 1 a.m. when you're half asleep and reach for the first thing on the nightstand...

RECEIPT

Book   9.99
Book   8.99
Book   9.99
Book   6.99
Book   5.99
Book   9.99

TOTAL:
$$$$$$

Any old piece of paper

A pen

Your glasses

DIARY

Another book

A spoon

A feather

The cat

# DESIGN A BRILLIANT BOOKMARK
# AND AN EXCELLENT EX LIBRIS

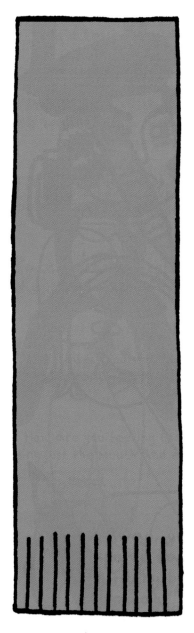

An *Ex Libris*, or bookplate, usually features a name, motto, or motif relating to the book's owner.

Try doodling your own bookmark and Ex Libris. Here are some examples to get you started.

# READING NOOK ESSENTIALS

A comfy, cozy place just for reading...what could be better? Here are a few essential items for the perfect reading nook.

A pillow

HOME sweet HOME

Good Lighting
(from a window or a lamp)

A big, comfortable chair

A small animal
of some kind

Plants

Snuggly
socks

...and lots and lots
of books of course!

An endless supply of
tea or coffee

# READING POSITIONS

Standard

Standard
with Leg curl

Sideways

Inverted

# DRAW A BEAUTIFUL BOOKCASE

1. Draw a rectangle. Make it as tall as you want your bookcase to be.

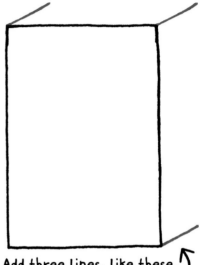

2. Add three lines, like these, to these three corners.

3. Join the lines with two straight ones.

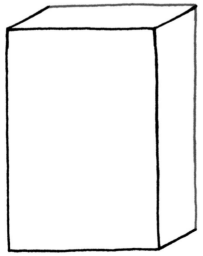

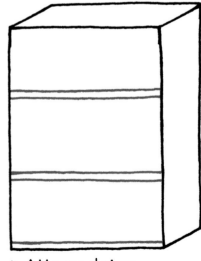

4. Add some shelves.

5. Now you can add some books! Draw spines of varying heights and widths on each shelf.

6. To make the books look 3-D, add angled lines at the top corners of the book spines, like this.

7. Well done! You've drawn a bookcase. Color the spines, and add the titles of your favorite books.

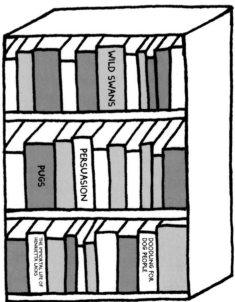

WILD SWANS

PUGS

PERSUASION

THE IMMORTAL LIFE OF HENRIETTA LAKS

DOODLING FOR DOG PEOPLE

# NONFICTION

## BIOGRAPHIES, MEMOIRS, AND AUTOBIOGRAPHIES

THE STORY OF MY LIFE

HELEN KELLER

I KNOW WHY THE CAGED BIRD SINGS

MAYA ANGELOU

Biography covers often feature an image of the subject...

MY FAMILY AND OTHER ANIMALS

GERALD DURRELL

THE DIVING BELL AND THE BUTTERFLY

JEAN-DOMINIQUE BAUBY

or images of important motifs, places, or objects.

Design a cover for a biography of your favorite person, animal, snack food, or whatever...

# FABULOUS FICTIONAL PLACES

Souvenir snowglobes from some literary landmarks.

Alex's home in
*A Clockwork Orange*

MUNICIPAL FLAT BLOCK
18A, LINEAR NORTH

Lavender
Rooms

THE EDMONT HOTEL
NEW YORK CITY

A hotel that Holden
checks into in
*A Catcher in the Rye*

Heathcliff's home in
(you've guessed it)
*Wuthering Heights*

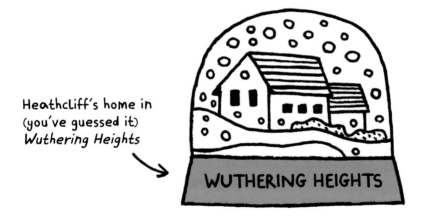

WUTHERING HEIGHTS

Try doodling your own fave fictional spots.

# DRAW A QUALITY QUILL & INK BOTTLE

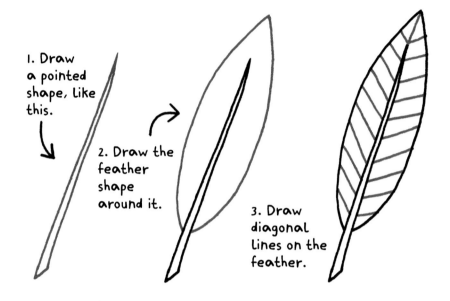

1. Draw a pointed shape, like this.

2. Draw the feather shape around it.

3. Draw diagonal lines on the feather.

## Now for the ink bottle...

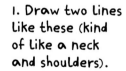

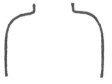

1. Draw two lines like these (kind of like a neck and shoulders).

2. Join the lines together at the bottom with a curved line, like this.

3. Add a rectangle shape at the top for a lid.

4. Add lines to the lid.

5. Draw a label for the bottle.

...and you're done!

6. Fill the bottle with ink!

# FUN LITERARY FACTS

**Fact:** *À la recherché du temps perdu,* by Marcel Proust, is the longest book in the world, at a whopping 9,609,000 characters.

**Fact:** John Steinbeck's puppy, Toby, ate the original manuscript for *Of Mice and Men.*

**Fact:** Isaac Asimov is the only author to have published a book in all 10 Dewey Library categories: General References or Works; Philosophy, Psychology, and Logic; Religion; Social Sciences; Language; Natural Science; Technology and Applied Science; Fine Arts and Recreation; Literature; and History and Biography.

**Fact:** The smallest book in the Welsh National Library, *Old King Cole,* measures 1mm x 1mm; its pages can only be turned with a needle!

**Fact:** Roald Dahl, author of *Charlie and the Chocolate Factory,* was a taste-tester for Cadbury chocolates as a schoolboy.

**Fact:** Oscar Wilde was given three middle names when he was born. His full name is Oscar Fingal O'Flahertie Wills Wilde.

**Fact:** Geoffrey Chaucer was the first poet to be buried in Westminster Abbey, initiating the Poet's Corner.

**Fact:** The first book that Dr. Seuss wrote and illustrated, *And to Think That I Saw It on Mulberry Street*, was rejected 27 times before it was published in 1937.

**Fact:** Edgar Allen Poe coined the word *tintinnabulation* in his poem, "The Bells." The word means "the sound of ringing bells."

**Fact:** George Eliot's real name was Mary Ann Evans.

**Fact:** The youngest recipient of the Nobel Peace Prize for Literature to date is Rudyard Kipling, best known for *The Jungle Book*. He was 42 years old when he was awarded the prize in 1907.

**Fact:** Samuel Clemens's pen name, Mark Twain, comes from a term that signifies two fathoms (12 feet) — a safe depth of water for steamboats.

# BOOKISH MERCHANDISE

Great gifts for the book lover in your life
(or yourself).

## T-SHIRTS

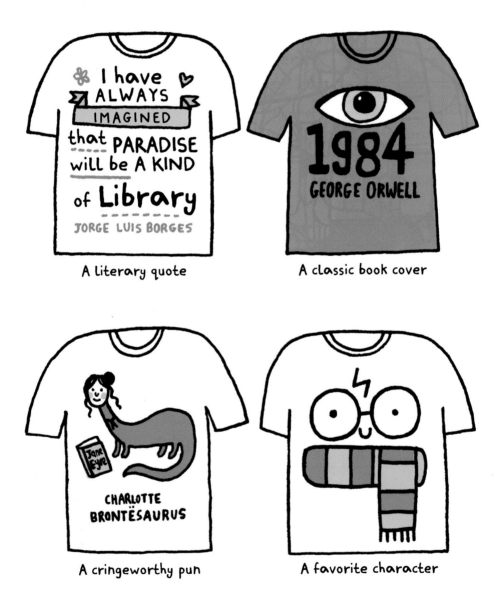

A literary quote

A classic book cover

A cringeworthy pun

A favorite character

## ACCESSORIES

A handy tote bag →

SO MANY BOOKS, SO LITTLE TIME!

← Bookworms!

## CERAMICS

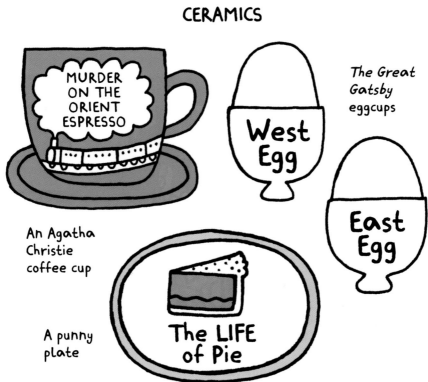

MURDER ON THE ORIENT ESPRESSO

The Great Gatsby eggcups

West Egg

East Egg

An Agatha Christie coffee cup

A punny plate

The LIFE of Pie

# LITERARY AROMAS

Scented candles inspired by aromas from classic books

RIPE WHEAT

from *O Pioneers!*

BURNING BOOKS

from *Fahrenheit 451*

PEMBERLEY GARDEN

from *Pride and Prejudice*

FRYING SAUSAGES AND SWEAT

from *Oliver Twist*

AMORTENTIA

from the Harry Potter Series

HAWTHORNE AND PLUM BLOSSOM

from *The Great Gatsby*

THE STREETS OF PARIS

from *Les Misérables*

BAKED STUFFED FISH AND SOUR RYE BREAD

from *Macbeth*

Try coming up with your own bookish scents!

# AMAZING BOOKSTORES

Every bibliophile knows that the best thing about visiting a new city is finding its best bookshops.

SHAKESPEARE AND COMPANY — Paris, France

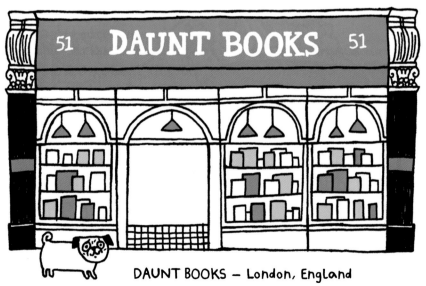

DAUNT BOOKS — London, England

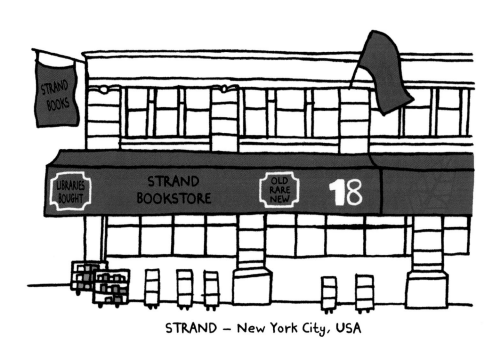

STRAND — New York City, USA

Do you have a favorite bookstore? Try doodling it!

BOOKS

THE CHEEKY PUG
BOOKSTORE

Black
Cat
BOOKS

Try designing a bookshop sign of your own!

# SHAKESPEARE

Prithee, what kind of book about books would this be without a Shakespeare section?

Here are a few of Mr. Shakespeare's best (and most fun to draw) characters.

OPHELIA
*Hamlet*

BOTTOM
*A Midsummer
Night's Dream*

PUCK
*A Midsummer
Night's Dream*

Alas, poor
YORICK
*Hamlet*

# SHAKESPEAREAN INSULTS

Bill sure knew how to write a witty put-down!

"Out, you green-sickness carrion!"

Lord Capulet
*Romeo and Juliet*

"Thou crusty batch of nature."

Achilles
*Troilus and Cressida*

"Away, you cut-purse rascal! You filthy bung, away!"

Doll Tearsheet
*Henry IV, Part II*

# CREATE YOUR OWN SHAKESPEAREAN INSULTS
## Choose a word from each column!

Thou...

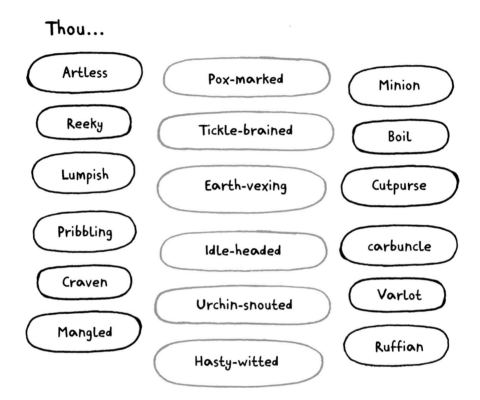

Artless

Pox-marked

Minion

Reeky

Tickle-brained

Boil

Lumpish

Earth-vexing

Cutpurse

Pribbling

Idle-headed

carbuncle

Craven

Urchin-snouted

Varlot

Mangled

Hasty-witted

Ruffian

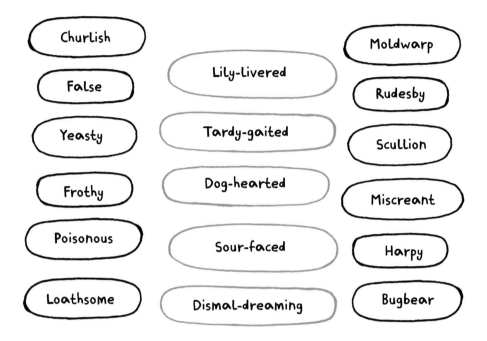

Churlish

False

Yeasty

Frothy

Poisonous

Loathsome

Lily-livered

Tardy-gaited

Dog-hearted

Sour-faced

Dismal-dreaming

Moldwarp

Rudesby

Scullion

Miscreant

Harpy

Bugbear

# NAME THAT BOOK!

Can you unscramble each of the words below
to find the single-word book title?
Hint: They're all considered classics.

1. TVLEILET:

2. ECABECR:

3. EIDAKNPDP:

4. RIOSSNPUEA:

5. OAENHIV:

6. LSUESYS:

7. FEONNIR:

8. MAIMRDHCLDE:

9. LAWDNE:

10. LHMAET:

11. OEBFUWL:

12. TOLILA:

13. ENSRKNTFNIAE:

14. APIOUT:

15. RLDUAAC:

# DRAW THE WONDERFUL WILLIAM SHAKESPEARE

1. Draw this shape.

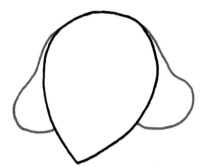

2. Add shapes like this for the hair.

3. Draw his eyes.

4. Next draw his nose and eyebrows.

5. Add a jaunty mustache!

6. Draw his mouth and the beard.

7. Draw his ear (and his hoop earring!).

8. Give him a classic Elizabethan ruff.

O proper stuff!
Thou hast made a fine work of art.

Rest you merry!

# PERFECT POETRY

But I, being poor,
have only my dreams;
I have spread my dreams
under your feet;
Tread softly because you
tread on my dreams.

from "Aedh Wishes for
the Cloths of Heaven"

William Butler Yeats

I love you much (most beautiful darling)
more than anyone on the earth and I
like you better than everything in the sky

E.E. Cummings

Hope is the thing with feathers
That perches in the soul,
And sings the tune
without the words,
And never stops at all.

Emily Dickinson

How doth the little crocodile
Improve his shining tail,
And pour the waters of the Nile
On every golden scale!

How cheerfully he seems to grin
How neatly he spreads his claws,
And welcomes little fishes in,
With gently smiling jaws!

Lewis Carroll

Write out some of your favorite pieces of poetry,
and doodle decorative borders for them.

There was an old man in a tree,
Who was horribly bored by a bee.
When they said,
"Does it buzz?"
He replied,
"Yes, it does!
It's a regular brute of a bee!"

Edward Lear

There was an old person
in gray,
Whose feelings were tinged
with dismay;
She purchased two parrots,
And fed them with carrots,
Which pleased that old person
in gray.

Edward Lear

# POETRY PRIMER

There are lots of poem types, from short to long.
Here's a quick guide to some of the more
popular forms.

**Acrostic**  A poem in which the first letter of each
line spells out a word, name, or phrase when read
vertically

**Aubade**  A love poem or song welcoming or lamenting
the arrival of the dawn

**Ballad**  A popular narrative song passed down
orally

**Couplet**  A pair of successive rhyming lines, usually
of the same length

**Epic**  A long narrative poem in which a heroic
protagonist engages in an action of great mythic
or historical significance

**Epigram**  A pithy, often witty poem

**Free verse**  Nonmetrical, nonrhyming lines that
closely follow the natural rhythms of speech

**Haiku** A Japanese form of three unrhyming lines in five, seven, and five syllables

**Limerick** A humorous rhyming poem of five lines

**Madrigal** A song or short lyric poem intended for multiple singers

**Octave** An eight-line stanza or poem

**Ode** A formal, often ceremonious lyric poem that addresses and often celebrates a person, place, thing, or idea

**Palinode** An ode or song that retracts or recants what the poet wrote in a previous poem

**Quatrain** A four-line, rhyming stanza

**Villanelle** A French verse form consisting of five three-line stanzas and a final quatrain, with the first and third lines of the first stanza repeating alternately in the following stanzas

# LITERARY GLOSSARY

**Anastrophe**  An inversion of the usual syntactical order of words for rhetorical effect

**Aphorism**  A terse saying embodying a general truth or astute observation

**Bibliophage**  An ardent reader; a bookworm!

**Book-bosomed**  A phrase coined by Sir Walter Scott to describe someone who carries a book at all times

**Bucolic**  A pastoral poem

**Clerihew**  A form of humorous verse, consisting of two couplets of metrically irregular lines, containing the name of a well-known person

**Deus ex machine**  A character or thing that suddenly enters the story and solves a problem that previously seemed impossible to solve

**Doggerel**  Bad verse characterized by loose or irregular measure; often comical

**Enjambment**  The running on of a thought from one line, couplet, or stanza to the next without a syntactical break

**Ex Libris**  A Latin phrase meaning "from the books" (or "from the library or collection of"); frequently used on bookplates

**Flyleaf**  A blank leaf or leaves inserted during the binding process between the free endpaper and the beginning or end of the printed pages

**Holographic**  Wholly written by the person in whose name it appears

**Incunabulum**  A book printed before 1501

**Kenning**  A conventional poetic phrase used for or in addition to the usual name of a person or thing

**Litote**  An understatement in which an affirmative is expressed by the negative of its contrary

**Logophile**  A lover of words

**Lucubrate**  To work, write, or study laboriously, especially at night

**Metonymy**  A figure of speech that consists of the use of the name of one object or concept for that of another to which it is related or a part of

**Neologism**  A new word, meaning, usage, or phrase

**Palindrome**  A word, phrase, or sentence that reads the same backward and forward

**Periphrasis**  The use of an unnecessarily long or roundabout form of expression

**Prosody**  The science or study of poetic meters and versification

**Recto**  The right-hand page of an open book or manuscript

**Rubric**  A title, heading, or the like in a book written or printed in red or otherwise distinguished from the rest of the text

**Sesquipedalian**  Given to or characterized by the use of long words

**Spoonerism*** The transposition of initial or other letters of words, usually by accident, as in *Runny Babbit: A Billy Sook* instead of *Bunny Rabbit: A Silly Book*

**Verso** The left-hand page of an open book or manuscript

**Quixotic** Resembling or befitting Don Quixote; extravagantly chivalrous or romantic; visionary, impractical, or impulsive

**Zeugma** The use of a word to modify or govern two or more words when it is appropriate to only one or to each but in a different way, as in "to wage war and peace"

*Try to come up with your own quirky spoonerisms!

Magnificent!

# FINISH THE LINE

Finish the opening lines to these famous novels—you can be true to the story...or you can put your own twist on things!

It is a _____ universally acknowledged that a single _____ in possession of a good _____ must be in want of a _____.

Jane Austen, *Pride and Prejudice*

Many years later, as he faced the _____, Colonel Aureliano Buendía was to remember that distant _____ when his _____ took him to discover _____.

Gabriel García Márquez, *One Hundred Years of Solitude*

It was a bright _____ day in _____, and the _____ were striking _____.

George Orwell, *1984*

It was the _____ of times, it was the _____ of times, it was the age of _____, it was the age of _____, it was the epoch of _____, it was the epoch of _____, it was the season of _____, it was the season of _____, it was the spring of _____, it was the winter of _____.

Charles Dickens, *A Tale of Two Cities*

Somewhere in _____, in a place whose name
I do not care to remember, a _____ lived
not long ago, one of those who has a _____
and ancient _____ on a shelf and keeps
a skinny _____ and a _____ for
racing.

Miguel de Cervantes, *Don Quixote*


_____ at a distance have every man's
_____ on board.

Zora Neale Hurston, *Their Eyes Were Watching God*


Under certain _____ there are few hours in
Life more _____ than the hour dedicated to
the _____ known as afternoon tea.

Henry James, *The Portrait of a Lady*


He was an old _____ who fished alone in
a _____ in the Gulf Stream and he had
gone _____ days now without taking a
_____.

Ernest Hemingway, *The Old Man and the Sea*

# POSTCARDS FROM FICTIONAL LANDS

Which of these places would you like to visit?

FOLLOW THE YELLOW BRICK ROAD

TO THE

EMERALD CITY

GREETINGS FROM NARNIA

# A DAY IN THE LIFE

From the break of dawn to the midnight hour, a day in the life of a bookworm is full of plot, intrigue, and imagination.

**6 AM** — Awaken after just a few hours of shut-eye...the fatigue is totally worth the late-night reading session to finish that favorite novel!

**6:30 AM** — Peruse bookshelf for the next big read...

**7 AM** — Read over morning breakfast and coffee (or tea!)

**8 AM** — Morning commute spent listening to a favorite audio book

**10:30 AM** — Mid-morning break for a snack and to update that ever-growing reading list...

**12 PM** — Lunch on a park bench—with a book in hand, obviously!

**2 PM** — Afternoon coffee break—just a drip coffee instead of the usual latte... gotta save those pennies for that new hardcover!

| 5 PM | Evening commute with a stop at the local bookstore to see what's new this week |
| 6:30 PM | Eat dinner while...you guessed it... reading |
| 7:30 PM | Write a glowing, anonymous online review of that guilty pleasure book you secretly read—and even more secretly loved |
| 8 PM | Three words: Bubble. Bath. Book. |
| 9:30 PM | In bed, happily reading away... |
| 10:30 PM | ..... |
| 11:30 PM | ..... |
| 12:30 PM | Finally fall asleep with the light still on... |

# LITERARY PUNS

Of course this book needs a section on puns, even if they have been called "the lowest form of humor." Shakespeare used puns, so they can't be that bad!

### ICE CREAM FLAVORS
### inspired by books

A CLOCKWORK ORANGE SORBET

THE RED VELVET TENT

REVOLUTIONARY
ROCKY ROAD

WAR
AND
PEACH

LITTLE
HOUSE ON
THE
PRALINE

BANANA
KARENINA

Try creating your
own literary
inspired flavors!

# FICTIONAL CHARACTER-INSPIRED PETS

BECKY SHARP CLAWS

HAIRY PAW-TER

JANE AIREDALE

ATTICUS FINCH

Your turn! Invent your own literary pet names.

# ABOUT THE ILLUSTRATOR

Gemma Correll is a cartoonist, writer, illustrator, and all-around small person. She is the author of *A Cat's Life, A Pug's Guide to Etiquette,* and *It's a Punderful Life,* among others. Her illustration clients include Hallmark, *The New York Times,* Oxford University Press, Knock Knock, Chronicle Books, and *The Observer.*
Visit www.gemmacorrell.com to see more of Gemma's work.